DRAWING
FROM MEMORY

DRAWING
FROM MEMORY

ALLEN SAY

SCHOLASTIC PRESS · NEW YORK

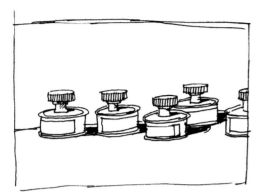

All rights reserved. Published by Scholastic Press, an imprint of Scholastic Inc., *Publishers since 1920*. SCHOLASTIC, SCHOLASTIC PRESS, and associated logos are trademarks and/or registered trademarks of Scholastic Inc.

CIP data available
ISBN 978-0-545-17686-6

10 9 8 7 6 5 4 3 2   12 13 14 15   Printed in Singapore 46
First edition, September 2011

The art for this book was created using watercolors, pen and ink, pencils, and photographs. Text was set in 13-point Monotype Fornier. Captions were set in a font created for this book based on Allen Say's handwriting. Book design by David Saylor and Charles Kreloff

Illustrations from *The Bicycle Man* by Allen Say (page 13 in this book, lower left) and (page 14 in this book, upper right) Copyright © 1982 by Allen Say. Reprinted by permission of Houghton Mifflin Harcourt Publishing Company. All rights reserved. Illustration from *The Sign Painter* by Allen Say (page 39 in this book, lower right) Copyright © 2000 by Allen Say. Reprinted by permission of Houghton Mifflin Harcourt Publishing Company. All rights reserved. Noro Shinpei cartoons that appear on pages 24, 29, 39, 50, 62 are reprinted by permission of Kunio Takama, executor of the estate of Noro Shinpei. Photographs that appear on pages 60, 61 are reprinted by permission of Kunio Takama. All other photographs are courtesy of the author.

FOR NINA IGNATOWICZ

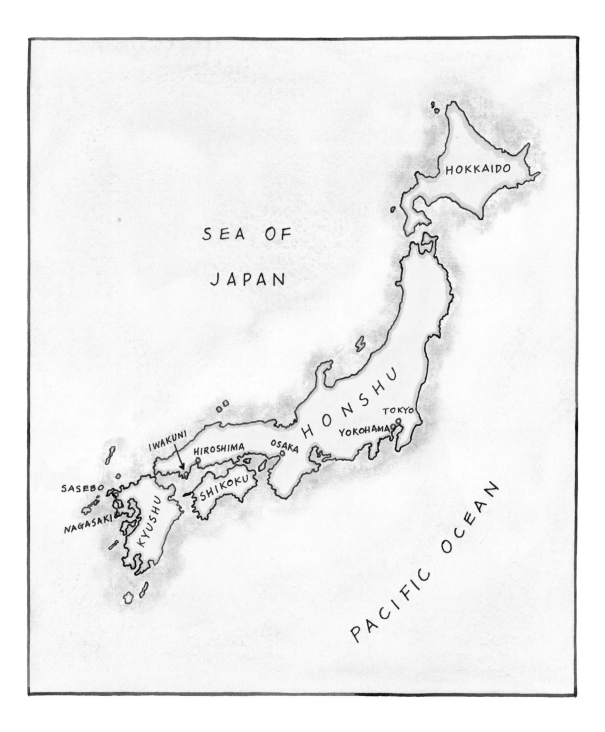

I WAS BORN IN 1937 BY THE SEASHORE OF YOKOHAMA, JAPAN.
Our house stood near a fishing village. My playmates were the children of fishermen. Mother constantly worried that I might drown in the sea. She tried to keep me at home.

She taught me to read before I started school, and that made me very popular among the neighborhood kids.

I could read comic books to them! I was like a little *kamishibai* man, a traveling storyteller with picture cards.

My mother's ploy worked. Comic books kept me at home. I read them for hours and stared at the pictures. I decided to become a cartoonist when I grew up.

So I drew.

I drew what I saw and what I imagined, and I copied from comic books.
When I was drawing, I was happy. I didn't need toys or friends or parents.

My parents were not pleased, especially
Father, who said, "I expect you to be a
respectable citizen, not an artist, and that
means you'll have to earn a living! Artists
are lazy and scruffy people—they are not
respectable."

TOKYO IN THE LATE 1930'S, AROUND THE TIME I WAS BORN

Every day, Father went to Tokyo to earn a living. I drew while he was away and hid my drawings when he came home.

Then a war began in 1941. When bombs started to fall on our city, Mother took us and fled to a village named Tabuse between Hiroshima and Iwakuni. Father stayed behind.

THE LAST PICTURE OF ME AND MY SISTER, SANAE, IN YOKOHAMA

We never went home again. My sister was two at the time and doesn't remember.

In the country, we stayed with Mother's uncle—the old man of the House of Moriwaki—who lived alone. He was mean and stingy and owned farmlands and mountains. For a whole year Sanae and I, and even Mother, tried to hide from him in his big house.

One day I would write a story about him in the language of the people who were bombing us. *Once Under the Cherry Blossom Tree* would be its title.

When the war ended four years later, everything was broken.

I WAS FOUR WHEN THE WAR BEGAN IN 1941. I AM WITH
MY BABYSITTER.

The American forces occupied Japan on my eighth birthday, August 28, 1945.
Our house in Yokohama had been destroyed. Father went to the south island of
Kyushu and found work in the city of Sasebo. We were reunited there.

I was sent to the local grammar
school and put in Mrs. Morita's
class. I was in first grade.

I'M IN THE MIDDLE OF THE TOP ROW.

YEARS LATER, I DREW MRS. MORITA
FROM MEMORY.

Mrs. Morita said that my ability to draw was a
wonderful talent. No one had told me that before.
She entered one of my drawings in a contest and it
won first place.

A SPORTS DAY SCENE AT SCHOOL THAT I HAD DRAWN FROM MEMORY

TWO AMERICAN SOLDIERS VISITED OUR SCHOOL ON THE FIRST SPRING SPORTS DAY AFTER THE WAR. ONE OF THEM DID ALL SORTS OF TRICKS ON THE PRINCIPAL'S BICYCLE. THIS IS A SKETCH OF THE MARINE WHO DID THE TRICK RIDING.

Japan and America were at peace now, but the marriage of our parents was broken. Father took me and my sister and left Mother. Soon we had a stepmother. She was a kind woman, but we missed our mother.

Mother returned to Yokohama and got a job and an apartment. I was eleven when she came to claim us. She took Sanae with her to Yokohama and sent me to stay with her mother in Tokyo. I was going into the sixth grade, time to prepare for middle school, and all the good schools were in Tokyo.

SANAE AND ME IN SASEBO A YEAR BEFORE MOTHER CAME FOR US. I'M TEN AND MY SISTER IS SIX.

Grandmother had lived alone until I came, and I made her unhappy.

"Drawing again!" she would say. "You'll never amount to anything!"

She sounded just like my father, who believed artists were unrespectable.

One day Grandmother said, "I have spoken with your mother. If you study hard and get accepted at Aoyama Middle School, we will let you live alone."

"What do you mean, Grandmother?" I asked.

"We will rent an apartment for you where you can be a serious student."

"Are you joking? I'm only twelve years old."

"I do not jest," she said.

I stared at Grandmother. She wasn't smiling, but she wasn't scowling, either.

Aoyama was a well-known private school, almost impossible to get into. But an apartment of my own! I quit drawing and studied for the first time.

I discovered that I had a good memory. I memorized names and dates, numbers and formulas, then took the Aoyama entrance examination.

On the day the school announced the exam results, Grandmother stayed home, so I went to find out by myself. At the school, the names of the students who had been accepted were posted on a big bulletin board. And there it was, my name leaping out at me. It seemed like the most beautiful name in the world. I called Mother at her office in Yokohama.

She was happy and relieved. "I can relax until you go to college," she said. She was already talking about my old age.

"Humph," Grandmother said when I told her. She was trying very hard not to smile. Next I told my sixth-grade teacher who had helped me so much to prepare for the examination.

"You make me proud to be a teacher!" he exclaimed.

MY SIXTH-GRADE TEACHER AND ME. I'M SORRY TO SAY I DON'T REMEMBER HIS NAME. I HOPE HIS RELATIVES WILL RECOGNIZE HIM.

Grandmother hired a man to move my things out of her house. As I left, she said, "Be sure to eat properly."

I was dazed with happiness as I marched to the place of my own. It was less than thirty minutes away from Grandmother's house, but it seemed like another world. It was springtime, just before my thirteenth birthday.

My room was in a "long house" known as the Eel's Bed, housing for the poor. As I opened the door this is what I saw. My own room! The bathroom door was on the left, the closet door was on the right.

I floated around the room all afternoon.

The one-room apartment was for me to study in,
but studying was far from my mind . . .

this was going to be my art studio!

I was still floating with joy when I went out that evening. I bought a newspaper, and that made me feel very grown up. I felt comfortable walking the bright busy streets of Tokyo. I was free in a safe city. I thanked Mother in my heart. She was supporting all of us—me, my sister, and Grandmother.

There were so many restaurants to choose from for my first dinner out, and I could order whatever I wanted to eat. *This is what it is to be an adult*, I thought. I wished I was finished with schooling. I couldn't wait to grow up.

I picked a plain restaurant, ordered my dinner, and read an article in the *Asahi* newspaper that made me forget to eat. It was about a boy three years older than me.

Here, I piece together the story I read in the paper and what the boy himself told me after we became friends:

In a high school in Osaka, a boy named Tokida drew pictures and did not study at all.

His father was not pleased. "No more comic books! No more drawing!" he yelled at his son.

Late that night, Tokida said good-bye to his home, to his school, and to the city of Osaka.

He walked at night and slept during the day, eating whatever he could find in the fields.

He reached Tokyo in sixteen days, went straight to a newspaper company, and made an announcement:

"My name is Tokida, and I want to be a cartoonist."

"How old are you?" someone asked.

"Fifteen."

"Where do you come from?"

"Osaka. I walked from there."

"That's about three hundred and fifty miles!"

"This is interesting," said the editor in chief of the paper.

The next morning, Tokida was front-page news. And just before noon, a man in a kimono came to the newsroom.

He was Noro Shinpei, one of the most famous cartoonists in Japan. He said to Tokida, "I will teach you if you like." Tokida couldn't believe his good fortune. He kept nodding yes, then fainted away.

So, like me, there was another boy who wanted to be a cartoonist! And he had Noro Shinpei, my favorite cartoonist, for his sensei, which means "teacher" or "master." Could I have walked sixteen days, with no money, for anything? I didn't eat the dinner I had ordered. When I got back to my room, it felt cold and lonesome.

FROM *GOLD MOUNTAIN* BY NORO SHINPEI, 1949

Noro Shinpei! My favorite cartoonist! He took on a student—a poor boy from Osaka only three years older than me!

I had been reading his comic strips since I was in Mrs. Morita's class. His books were my secret treasures I hid from my parents. They had the first dinosaurs I'd ever seen, and there were a lot of wild animals and boy heroes and supernatural bad men, all fighting one another. But I liked his horses best and copied them in my school notebooks. Mother used to shake her head but didn't tell Father.

By the time I moved to Tokyo, Noro Shinpei's style had changed. The scary characters disappeared, and dinosaurs were replaced by *kappas*. His serials were very funny now. And he started to put himself in some of his stories, usually dressed like a monk with wild hair.

Would the great man take on another student? I wondered.

KAPPAS ARE CREATURES OF LEGEND IN JAPANESE FOLKLORE. ABOUT THE SIZE OF CHILDREN, THEY HAVE SCALES ON THEIR ARMS AND LEGS, WEBBED FEET, AND SHELLS ON THEIR BACKS LIKE TORTOISES. THEY LIVE IN RIVERS AND PONDS, AND ARE MISCHIEVOUS TROUBLEMAKERS.

I had two whole weeks before I started in my new school. And on the first day, I went looking for my sensei. I had the address from the newspaper article about Tokida, and it didn't take me long to find the place. The drab building depressed me, and I wasn't sure if I should go in.

On the last door in the building, a name card was pinned below the glass. I read the four characters several times. *Noro Shinpei, Noro Shinpei, Noro Shinpei!* I tapped on the glass.

"Enter!" a man's voice ordered.

The great cartoonist wasn't an old man. I recognized Tokida from the newspaper article. He didn't look very friendly.

"Come in and tell us who you are," said the master.

I gave him my last name. "Sei, sir."

"Unusual name. How do you write that?"

I told him.

"Kiyoi." He mispronounced the two characters of my family name. I'd never been called Kiyoi before, but I didn't have the nerve to correct him. Besides, I liked how it sounded.

"Should I guess the nature of your errand?"

"I want to be a cartoonist, sir."

Tokida made a sound like a snort. The shirt collar tightened around my neck and I started to sweat.

"How old are you?" Master Noro asked.

"Almost thirteen, sir."

He looked me up and down, then asked all sorts of questions. I lied that my parents were together and didn't mention Grandmother or my apartment.

"Why do you want to be a cartoonist?"

I wasn't prepared for that question from a cartoonist!

"I don't know . . . drawing is all I want to do, sir."

"Ah, a boy Hokusai, mad about drawing. All right, draw something for me . . . let's say a horse." He handed me a drawing pad. He was comparing me to Hokusai, the great Japanese painter who called himself "Old Man Mad About Drawing"!

THE TOP CHARACTER MEANS "PURE" OR "CLEAR"; THE BOTTOM IS A WELL. TOGETHER, THEY CAN BE READ AS "SEII" OR "KIYOI."

This was scarier than the Aoyama Middle School entrance exam! That was only for an apartment. Now I was taking the test to decide my whole future as an artist, the only future I wanted. *Remember all the horses you'd copied from Noro Shinpei's comics. Give one back now!*

When I sat down to draw, suddenly I was alone in the room. With a pencil and paper, I didn't feel afraid anymore. The horse came out something like this. Sensei looked at it politely.

"What if I don't take you on as an apprentice?" the cartoonist asked.

"I don't know . . . I'll do it on my own, sir."

The room swayed around me. . . . I thought I was drowning until I heard Sensei's laugh.

"Meet Tokida, your new partner."

Tokida gave me a slow nod.

"I can be your pupil, sir?"

"If that's what you want. But no mention of tuition, is that clear? I'm not running a school here."

"Yes, sir."

"And one more thing, Kiyoi, always carry a sketchbook and use it."

I bowed to them and walked out into the world with a name of my own. Kiyoi! I didn't tell Father, or anyone else, either.

I went back the next morning.

"Just in time for your first combat," Sensei said. "Three o'clock deadline. Tokida will show you what to do."

"Pull up a chair." Tokida spoke to me for the first time. He handed me a bristol board and said, "Fill in the sky."

A panel of Sensei's original drawings!

"With ink?" I asked.

"Remember, it's wet."

He told me to put a piece of paper under my hand and work from left to right so I wouldn't smudge the ink. This was the scariest of all—putting my hands on the master's original work!

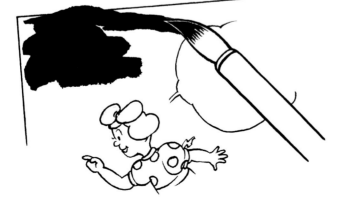

The brush went where it liked no matter how hard I gripped it. It *was* like a combat.

"Don't fret, Kiyoi, watch Tokida," Sensei said.

Tokida dipped a brush in white paint and covered up the mess I'd made. "Keep going," Tokida told me.

So I did.

"Very good, Kiyoi," Sensei said. "The brush is many things. You just used it like a knife. Remember that edge."

"Yes, sir." I struggled through the first board.

Then it was my turn to watch Sensei.

He drew fast—first with a pencil, then with a dip pen. When the ink dried, I got to erase the pencil lines, and the figures I'd seen in magazines and newspapers leaped out at me. While waiting for the next board, I sharpened pencils and poured tea.

THIS IS SENSEI'S BEST-KNOWN COMIC BOOK CHARACTER, DEMOKURASHEE-CHAN, OR SHEE-CHAN FOR SHORT. DEMOCRACY WAS A STRANGE NEW WORD IN JAPAN AFTER THE WAR, AND SENSEI USED IT AS THE NAME OF A GIRL IN A COMIC SERIAL FOR A CHILDREN'S NEWSPAPER. BEFORE SHEE-CHAN CAME ALONG, ALMOST ALL THE MAIN CARTOON CHARACTERS WERE BOYS.

A week after I started, Sensei rented a suite in an old inn. "Our new fort, with room service," he said. It was the kind of place I had imagined the master to be working in. Tokida slept in one of the rooms. Sensei had another apprentice, named Kubota-san. He was a college student who was a couple of years older than Tokida. We didn't see him often.

Sensei drew the characters and the speech balloons. Tokida put in the backgrounds. I inked the skies and hairdos and clothing. There was no other place in the world I wanted to be.

Sensei was treated like a lord, and Tokida and I were princes. Maids brought up food and tea all hours of the day.

For Sensei, the inn was his studio. When he didn't have to work at night, he went home to his family. He and his wife had two children.

Sometimes Sensei had visitors—magazine editors, photographers, other cartoonists. He took all of us to a coffeehouse he liked. I sat and listened to famous men talk and felt like a celebrity myself.

One day Sensei left in the early afternoon. "Come on, Kiyoi." Tokida hopped out the window and crawled up to the roof. The height scared me but I followed. He loosened pieces of dried clay from under the roof tiles and threw them as far as he could. Then he coaxed me to throw some, too. As someone shouted from below, we scuttled back to our room.

After a good laugh, we spread out the finished panels to admire the work we had done during the day.

"Let's sign our names on them," Tokida said.

"We can't do that!" I said.

"Just make them small . . . one letter here, one letter there. Nobody will ever know."

We were signing our names when a maid brought us tea and cakes. She thought we were doing serious work.

When all the panels had our names hidden in them, Tokida and I sketched each other.

Then we went out to draw the real world. Even though I was three years younger, I was taller than Tokida. He resented that. We stopped at the coffeehouse Sensei had taken us to. The waitresses remembered us—the young cartoonists!—but when school started, I was only a middle-school student.

KINGYO (MISS GOLDFISH, SECOND ROW FROM BOTTOM, FAR LEFT)

MISS SAITO

In the fall of 1950 I was still in my first year at Aoyama. I wasn't a good student. It was depressing to count the years before I could be a cartoonist. It was like a prison sentence.

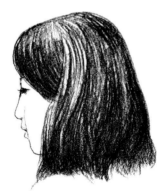

A GIRL I ADMIRED IN ANOTHER CLASS

There was an army of teachers who loaded us down with homework. I envied Tokida, a high-school dropout, who could stay at the inn, the great school of cartooning!

There was romance among the teachers, but students weren't allowed to date. I would have to date secretly, but the girl I liked was in another class. So what good was school? I already had a master who taught me everything I needed to know. Why was I there?

But I made two good friends—an art teacher we called Miss Goldfish, and Miss Saito, who taught music.

I HAD FUN DRAWING CARICATURES OF TEACHERS.

ME, MISS GOLDFISH, ORITO-SAN

Miss Goldfish introduced me to her former student named Orito, who was preparing for the entrance exam to the famous Tokyo School of Fine Arts. He was three years older than me and already an amazing artist. After classes, Goldfish let him use the art room for a studio. Soon Orito-san took me on as his studio mate.

There, Orito-san taught me to draw from Greek and Roman sculptures, using charcoal sticks and erasing with wads of fresh bread.

The idea was to draw like Michelangelo, which was impossible. I made a lot of black smearing, wasted charcoal and paper, and ate most of the eraser. I didn't understand how Orito-san could make a drawing look so real, like a photograph.

"Spend a month on a drawing," he told me.

"Same sheet of paper?"

"The same," he said.

The first sculpture I tried drawing was Venus de Milo. How to render a pure white statue on a piece of white paper with a stick of black charcoal? It was a mess. Spend six months? Maybe a year? Maybe forever.

Then there was the bust of Brutus, with all the folds in the robe. And I could spend a whole month just on David's messy hair. Michelangelo had made them both!

BRUTUS

DAVID

33

One day I caught Orito-san by himself doing what looked like a strange, furious dance. He was practicing karate. I'd thought only gangsters and professional killers knew karate. I asked if he would teach me. "Sure," Orito-san said. "Artists should be able to defend themselves."

Orito-san considered me an artist! And our art room became our dojo, a place to practice the deadly martial art. It was like the clubhouse of a secret society with only two members.

Wait till Father hears about this, I thought. Maybe he wouldn't think I was such a sissy anymore. But I was glad I lived far away from him. He had a new family now.

I'd been living in Tokyo for over a year. Mother came up from Yokohama once a month to visit. Each time we had a get-together at Grandmother's house, where my sister was staying now. I'd been waiting for a chance to tell Mother about Sensei, but Grandmother was always scowling nearby.

Finally, I went to the office where Mother worked and she took me out to lunch. Just Mother and me. We hadn't done that since I was a little boy. I felt nervous, as if I were on an interview.

"Is it tuition, then?" Mother asked.

"There's no tuition, Mother. I'm one of Sensei's three assistants. Is that all right?"

"You've always drawn, son, and I think I've learned a lesson from the old saying, 'Let your dear child journey.' I'm only concerned about your schoolwork."

"I'll study hard, Mother, I promise. Could you tell Grandmother about all of this? I'll write to Father."

"Don't worry about Grandmother. She means well. I'm very happy for you, son, to have such a kind sensei. Do thank him for me."

I was grinning all the way home. People stared at me but I didn't care. And I didn't write to Father. He wasn't the one who was supporting me. Why should I tell him anything?

One afternoon in early spring of 1951, as I was drawing in the art room at school, a strange thing happened. My eyeball floated up to the ceiling and watched me drawing down below. It didn't seem crazy until the eyeball returned to my head. It was like waking from a dream, or maybe I was sleep-drawing. There on the easel was the best drawing of Brutus or of any statue I had ever made. And I didn't know how I did it. I took it to show Sensei.

"Well done, Kiyoi, beautiful grays," he said. "You've discovered the world between black and white."

Tokida said nothing. His silence made me very nervous.

"But I can't draw hands, Sensei. How long do I have to practice?" I asked.

THESE ARE FROM AN OLD SKETCHBOOK FROM THAT PERIOD, THE ONLY SKETCHBOOK I DIDN'T BURN WHEN I LEFT JAPAN.

THE KARATE FIST WAS EASY—NO FINGERS!

"Bad word, Kiyoi. Drawing is never a practice. To draw is to see and discover. Every time you draw, you discover something new. Remember that."

"Yes, sir."

"Kiyoi should be drawing real people," Tokida said.

"You are right," Sensei agreed. "Tokida and Kubota have been taking a life drawing class, and it's time you join them."

That meant drawing nude models. My face flushed.

KUBOTA-SAN AND TOKIDA

Kubota-san, the college student, wanted to be a serious painter. He had been taking the figure drawing class long before Tokida started.

THE FIRST GOOD PHOTO I TOOK WITH MY CAMERA, A PRESENT FROM MOTHER, WAS A PICTURE OF KUBOTA-SAN AND HIS MOTHER. LIKE ALL GOOD PICTURES, IT WAS AN ACCIDENT. I DIDN'T THINK PHOTOGRAPHY WAS ART—YOU DIDN'T HAVE TO DRAW HANDS.

Tokida took me to my first life drawing class. "Sit down and start drawing," he hissed in my ear.

I watched him draw, and he kept hissing. What I discovered was how clumsy I was, and how hard it was to draw a naked human body! But I did get used to looking at the model.

"Don't worry about the face or hands or feet," Tokida told me. "Concentrate on the outline and volume—you know, the whole form."

He sounded as if we were drawing a horse. My figures looked like rag dolls with no clothes on. I burned the sketchbook the next day.

I DREW THESE A YEAR LATER.

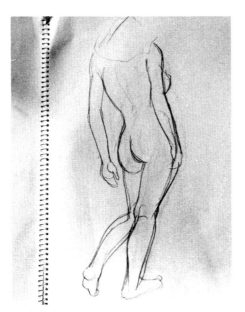

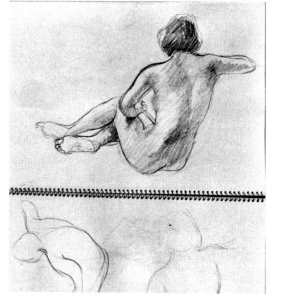

PESO, THE DOG, ME AS KYUSUKE (WITH BACKPACK), AND TOKIDA (IN BLACK JACKET) AS TANPEI

That summer, Sensei introduced two new characters in his "Demokurashee-chan" comic strip—Tokida and me! He even gave us new names—Tanpei for Tokida, Kyusuke for me. The frame at the top is the first one of the serial.

Each story was a cliff-hanger. Along with Shee-chan, a dog named Peso, and Sensei himself, we got into all sorts of trouble but we were always saved for the next adventure. It was like being in movies with famous stars.

SAVED BY A KAPPA

ME TRAVELING IN AMERICA A FEW YEARS LATER

In the summer of 1951, Father invited me to his house in Sasebo but I didn't go. Instead, Tokida and I spent a lot of time exploring the big world of Tokyo. We felt like Tanpei and Kyusuke, our comic book doubles.

"Look at them," Tokida said. "They all go to offices and do the same thing every day until they die. I'll never work for anybody. If I can't be a cartoonist, I'll shine shoes."

"I won't get a job, either," I said. "I'll shine shoes with you."

In an art gallery in the Ginza, the main shopping area, we saw real Van Gogh paintings for the first time. Tokida got very excited.

"Van Gogh painted with his fingers!" he said.

"No he didn't! I can see the brush marks."

"How can you see anything in this mob! We didn't come to see a baseball game. Let's get out of here!"

"Office slaves!" Tokida fumed outside. "Look, they're too lazy to shine their own shoes. I won't do it! I'll never shine their shoes! I'll starve first."

"I won't, either," I said.

We tried to draw people on the streets.

STREET MUSICIAN

SANDWICH MAN

ESCALATOR WOMAN

FORTUNE-TELLER

SHOP BOY

TOFU SELLER

MONK BEGGING FOR ALMS

GIRLS SELLING FLOWERS

NOODLE DELIVERY MAN

WOMEN DRESSED FOR TEA CEREMONY

POLITICIAN

Even though many of them looked like characters out of comic books, it was hard to capture them in our sketchbooks. I felt jealous of photographers who could sneak up on strangers and snap their pictures on the run. But that seemed like hunting and stealing.

We were near the Ginza when we heard the roaring of a mob.

"Let's go see," Tokida said.

"It's a riot," I said.

"Don't be stupid, it's only a demonstration."

He pulled me toward the commotion.

A huge crowd was getting into a marching formation, shouting in a chorus. Soon Tokida was shouting with them. I wanted to run but we were already stuck in the sea of humans.

Office workers, college students, and tradesmen turned into a human train and we couldn't get off it. We snaked down the boulevard. To ease my fear, I shouted with them.

THE POLICE WERE WAITING FOR US.

There were strikes every month. They were about injustice. The jobless people wanted work; poor workers wanted more money; university students wanted books and a better education. They demonstrated for a better government, for a better world. The police beat them down.

Tokida looked around my room.

"Where are your parents?"

"They are divorced."

He stared. "Only American movie stars get divorced.

"Where do you eat? What do you do for money?"

"My mother supports me. Why don't you wash up and put this on."

I gave him a clean shirt.

"If I had a studio like this I'd never go out."

We talked until it got dark.

45

I didn't leave my room until the next night, when Tokida came to get me. People scared me now, ordinary people who could go mad in an instant. Tokida and I were in real danger yesterday. We weren't in a comic book adventure.

I was still angry with Tokida but didn't say anything.

COME ON, SENSEI IS TAKING US TO DINNER . . .

And I had my first dinner with Sensei.

"Tokida's got the Van Gogh fever," Sensei said. Tokida had not told Sensei about the demonstration.

"He painted everything in the same way, with the same strokes—trees, faces, everything," I said.

"Good point, Kiyoi. With Van Gogh, each brushstroke is like a word in a book. Painting is a kind of writing, and writing is a kind of painting—they are both about seeing."

I'd never heard anyone talk about painting and writing in that way. Listening to him, I forgot about the riot.

"Van Gogh didn't paint," Tokida said. "He raked the colors on the canvas. You can do that with your fingers."

"Violent paintings appeal to you." Sensei laughed. I looked at him. He didn't ask me when I had to be home, so Tokida must have told him I lived by myself.

After dinner, Sensei took us to an art store, where he introduced us to the manager.

"Kindly furnish them with oil-painting kits." Tokida gave me a nudge. I turned my face to hide the blushing. Carrying our treasures, we followed Sensei out as calmly as we could.

"Put them to good use," he told us. We kept bowing our thanks until Sensei said, "Enough."

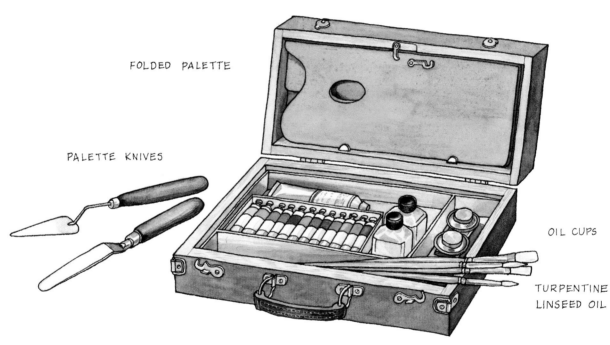

FOLDED PALETTE

PALETTE KNIVES

OIL CUPS

TURPENTINE
LINSEED OIL

Our paint boxes were probably fancier than the one Van Gogh had used. And Tokida and I might have looked a little like the great painter as we went out looking for scenes to paint that weekend.

I HOPE IT DOESN'T RAIN...

I'LL PAINT IF THERE'S A TYPHOON.

Actually, I only wanted to paint girls but didn't know where to start.

When I tried to talk to the girls, they giggled and walked away. *Are they ever interested in boys?*

In my second year I still didn't know most of the boys. They weren't interested in me, either.

So I studied. Maybe I could show those rich kids artists were as smart as anybody. My grades went up.

Miss Saito, the music teacher, often took me and Orito-san to her favorite coffeehouse.

I asked Orito-san if he would teach me to paint with oils. "Let's start with still life," he said.

"I love it, I must have it," said the music teacher. And she bought it from Orito-san! That's what I had to do. Paint a beautiful portrait of the girl I liked and give it to her!

That ought to impress her. But first I needed a picture of her to paint from.

And I finally got one on a school excursion. I had to include two of her friends, though, but I could cut them out later. . . . I had to wait a whole week for the pictures to be developed.

Once I got the photo back, it was out of focus.

The girl was fuzzier than my memory. I hated photography.

Before any girl would talk to me, I had to be daring and free like Kyusuke, my cartoon self. The girl would be Shee-chan, a cartoon heroine. And now that I was drawing some of the background they ran around in, I was living in a world I was making up—just what I had always wanted to do as a cartoonist. But I kept asking myself, *Will I ever have a real girlfriend?*

In the fall of 1952 I got a letter from my father, who still lived in Sasebo. Enclosed in the letter was a big check, and that made me nervous. Father was a businessman and money meant only one thing to him: business. Sure enough, he had a deal to make. He and his family were planning to immigrate to America and he wanted to know if I would like to go with them. All of a sudden he was including me in his family. I had to sit down.

What would Kyusuke do? I asked myself. He would grab his knapsack and go, and either a *kappa* or Sensei would always get him out of trouble. But I was in the real world. I had seen Father abandon Mother. Why would he save me from anything? I would have to stall him with my answer.

"Let's see if this is real, Kyusuke," I said, and took the check to a post office, where it turned into a bundle of real money. I went back to the art store Sensei had taken us to and spent all the cash on canvases and expensive French oil paints. It was the first time my father bought art supplies for me. I imagined the look on his face and it made me smile.

I told Sensei and Tokida the news.

"Wonderful," Sensei said in English.

"Why do you want to go to America?" Tokida asked.

"Why not?" Sensei said. "Traveling is the greatest teacher of all, so let your dear child journey."

That was the old saying I'd heard from Mother. *Is that how she really felt?* I wondered. It's just an old saying, after all.

"When is your old man going?" asked Tokida.

"In a year, maybe longer."

"Then you have time to think about it," Sensei said. "He can always go first and send for you later."

It was so simple! Why didn't Father give me that option?

When Sensei left the room, Tokida said, "Here's to your America," and shot an elastic band at me.

"What's this?" I asked.

"Something to hold the glasses on my head."

"I've never seen you wear it before."

"Only when I demonstrate."

"What? You're not rioting again!"

"Demonstrating!" he shouted.

I left the inn without saying good-bye to Tokida. If he wanted to riot, that was his business. I had freedom and opportunity already. Why would I want to go to America? I would have to live with my father there, and leaving Sensei

would be harder for me. But why was Father asking me to go with him? I didn't know what to think.

I went home and wrote Mother a letter, telling her about Father's offer.

The news excited her. A few days later, Mother and I had a get-together at Grandmother's house.

"I'm so happy for you!" Mother said.

"He is too young to leave home," Grandmother said.

She'd forgotten I'd been away two years. I was fifteen now. We talked in circles, and in the end Mother said the

decision to go to America was up to me. Grandmother agreed grudgingly. I could stay where I was or go to a strange country and be on my own. What to do?

Orito-san was the first one I told at school.

"You lucky guy!" he shouted.

"Would *you* go to America?"

"Like a bullet," he said. "Who wants to live on a crowded little island like this? Let me get through college first and I'll come join you. Count on it!"

He cheered me up. *Be decisive like Orito-san, the karate fighter! Be adventurous like Kyusuke!* I went to see Mother in Yokohama.

I wanted to catch her by surprise, to find out what she really thought. But she surprised me first. I saw her walking with a man I didn't know, and I ducked into a doorway. I'd never thought about Mother having suitors until now. Like Tokida and me, she had her own life to live. But she also had to support me, Sanae, and Grandmother.

As Mother and the man got into a taxi I thought about Father—he was my father, after all. Let him pay my way to the new country. That night I wrote him a letter: Yes, I would like to go to America with you.

I would go like Kyusuke. Mother would have one less to support.

The next ten months passed like a speeded-up movie. I looked hard at everything and tried to remember what I saw and felt. Soon all would be memories.

THREE YOUNG CARTOONISTS

AT AN INN ON A SCHOOL EXCURSION

OUR LAST FAMILY OUTING. HERE I AM WITH MY SISTER NEAR MT. FUJI.

WITH MISS GOLDFISH AT SCHOOL WINTER CAMP

MY MOTHER HAD A PRETTY SMILE.

WITH A CLASSMATE

A week before I left, Sensei took me and Tokida to what he called a "temporary farewell dinner."

"You are going to the great land of freedom," he said. "But remember that no man is entirely free of anything. Artists are bound to their art. Be true to your art, Kiyoi, and journey well."

"Show them how good you are," Tokida said, and he gave me a smile to remember.

"Good-bye, brother. Good-bye, Sensei." I was glad they didn't look back. I was sobbing in public.

By the end of the next day, my room was empty except for my drawings and sketchbooks. I took them out to the vacant yard and made a bonfire. In an hour they turned to ashes. I felt free, like Kyusuke.

I was leaving my apartment the way I'd found it three years before. It was like checking out of a room of an inn. And like Kyusuke, I was ready to start a new life with what I could carry on my back.

AUTHOR'S NOTE

"Let your dear child journey" is an old Japanese saying I first heard from my mother, who had no way of knowing that this book would let me journey through my memories of becoming an artist. *Drawing from Memory* has also allowed me to travel through the master/disciple relationship I enjoyed with Noro Shinpei, and my final reunion with this man who had become my spiritual father. Before he took me on, Noro, whom I called Sensei—a Japanese term for master or teacher—had often moved from one studio to the next to escape from magazine and newspaper editors who hounded him for his new work. But in the time I knew him, he had moved only once, from the small office where I first met him to the wonderful suite at the old inn. When his work was done, he went home to his wife and two children.

TAKEN IN 2000 BY CHIEKO-SAN, THE YOUNGER OF SENSEI'S TWO DAUGHTERS BY HIS FIRST WIFE. THIS WAS THE LAST TIME I SAW THE MASTER.

POSING FOR A MAGAZINE ARTICLE

SENSEI DRAWING FOR AN AUDIENCE

THE MASTER WITH *HIS* SKETCHBOOK

THIS IS THE ONLY DRAWING OF TOKIDA'S I OWN, AND I STOLE IT. I BELIEVE IT'S A SKETCH OF SENSEI'S FIRST WIFE, MASAKO.

The week I became his student, Sensei introduced me to his first wife, Masako-san, and their two daughters, Michiko and Chieko, about four and one respectively. That was the first and the last time I saw Masako-san. (In Japanese culture, putting "san" at the end of someone's name is a polite way of addressing that person—it is more casual than Mr., Mrs., Miss, or Ms. in English.)

In 2006, four years after Sensei died, Michiko and Chieko and I had a reunion in Tokyo, and I learned that all their family photographs had been destroyed and that they had no memory of their mother. I was the

SENSEI AND HIS SECOND WIFE, TOSHIKO, WITH THEIR DAUGHTER, SEIKO. HE IS HOLDING CHIEKO'S HANDS; MICHIKO IS ON THE RIGHT.

WITH THEIR SON, SHU.

only person they knew who remembered Masako-san. So for this book, I called back to my mind a face I had seen sixty years ago and drew it for them. My sketch, shown here, is the only clue they have in imagining what their mother looked like.

When I left Japan in July of 1953, the world was a bigger place than it is now— an easier place in which to get lost. I got to California, exchanged a few letters with Sensei and Tokida, and then fell out of contact with them. Three years later I returned to Yokohama, where my mother was living with her second husband and my sister. A day after my arrival, I went looking for Sensei, but this time I didn't have his address. As I got on a train to Tokyo, I felt calm, as though walking in my sleep, and I'm usually very nervous about everything. Somehow I felt certain I was going to find Sensei in a city of eight million people. And arriving there, for no particular reason, I picked one of the many city trains and got on. As I was pushed into the crowded car, I almost ran into Sensei. There he was, standing in the aisle in his usual kimono, holding on to a hand strap and carrying a sleeping baby in one arm. I started to bow to him.

"Ah, Kiyoi," he said, and gave me a nod. He acted as though we had seen each

I DREW THIS PICTURE OF SENSEI'S FIRST WIFE, MASAKO, FROM MEMORY. HER TWO DAUGHTERS, MICHIKO AND CHIEKO, DON'T REMEMBER HER.

TOKIDA TOOK OFF HIS GLASSES FOR THIS PHOTO. HE IS STANDING ON A ROCK BEHIND ME.

other just the day before, talking about an errand he had to run, or maybe it was about the weather. A few stations later, as the automatic doors opened, he said, "We get off here," and I followed him out. It was an area of Tokyo I didn't know.

He took me to his house and introduced me to his lovely new wife, Toshiko-san. Then he handed her their son, Shu, and went to order food and sake for a celebration.

"So you are Kiyoi-san," she said. "Last night, my husband called your name three times in his sleep."

When my editor, Andrea Pinkney, and I first talked about this book, she asked me if it was possible to include some of my master's work in it. The thought had never occurred to me; I didn't think any of Sensei's work could be found today. Without much expectation, I asked his daughter Chieko-san, and she went to the International Children's Library in Tokyo and dug up some ancient treasures! For me the most precious is on page 39 of this book, the opening frame of a serial in which Sensei introduces Tokida and me as Tanpei and Kyusuke. It went on to become a popular serial, but in my journey to find my place in America, I somehow forgot that once I was a comic book character. Life in the New World had erased a part of my past. It was Chieko-san who pointed out the similarity between Kyusuke and my later self-portrait in my picture book *The Sign Painter*: The same knapsack appears in both!

NORO SHINPEI'S LATER WORK ABOUT A SAMURAI BOY, *THE FLYING MONKEY*

The last time I saw him, Sensei was eighty-five years old. We met in a restaurant in Yugawara, a town at the foothills of Mt. Fuji, where a newspaper reporter ambushed us. I was furious, but the master kindly invited him to his apartment nearby. The reporter asked him, "What was Kiyoi-san like when he first came to you?"

Sensei replied, "He came to me as a man wearing a mask of a boy."

Looking back from where I am today, I see Sensei as a boy who wore a mask of a man.

When I finished the illustrations for this book, I sent Chieko-san the original drawing of her mother. She thanked me and wrote: "About one year before my father died at age eighty-seven, on February 20, 2002, I asked him if there was anything he wanted to do. He looked at me steadily and said, 'Kiyoi is the treasure of my life. I want to work on a book with him.'"

This is that book.

ALLEN SAY